AFRICAN STUDENTS
STUDYING IN AMERICA

AFRICAN STUDENTS STUDYING IN AMERICA

Their Experiences and Adjustment Problems at an HBCU

An Abridged version

DR. ANDREW C. BLAKE

iUniverse, Inc.
Bloomington

African Students Studying in America
Their Experiences and Adjustment Problems at an HBCU

iUniverse books may be ordered through booksellers or by contacting:

iUniverse
1663 Liberty Drive
Bloomington, IN 47403
www.iuniverse.com
1-800-Authors (1-800-288-4677)

ISBN: 978-1-4697-0634-4 (sc)
ISBN: 978-1-4697-0636-8 (ebk)

Printed in the United States of America

iUniverse rev. date: 01/18/2012

CONTENTS

Dedication vii
Introduction...1
What the literature shows..6
Brief history of Delaware State University 18
Ways the data were collected and treated 20
The results...24
Conclusions and recommendations 41
What the educational experiences of African
     students in America mean to us..........................52
References 53
Appendix...59

DEDICATION

This book is dedicated to my dear wife, Mogibloa, and my two children, Andrew, Jr. and Francess. A special gratitude is also extended to my uncle and his wife, Dr. Cecil and Mrs. Hortensia Blake.

CHAPTER I

Introduction

It is not a surprise to many that the international student population in the United States has increased exponentially over the years. While many other countries are known for admitting international students, the United States has the highest number of these students in the world (Institute of International Education, 2001). For example, in the 2001-2002 school year, there were 582,996 international students studying in the United States, and in the 2009-2010 school year, there were 690,923 international students enrolled in U.S. colleges (Institute of International Education, 2011). Statistics reveal that in the 2000-2001 school year, there were 34,217 African students enrolled at institutions of higher learning in the United States, and in the 2007-2008 school year, there were 35,654 African students in U.S. colleges (National Center for Educational Statistics). As the number of international students continues to rise, so do the challenges that the students have to deal with. For some, the issue is the unfamiliarity with the English language, and for others, it is the customs and traditions that they have to get accustomed to. The

1

fact, however, remains that students from other countries are extremely vital to U.S. colleges and universities because they contribute to the idea of the "melting pot," bring added cultural richness to the institutions, and contribute billions of dollars to the U.S. economy. Examples of some of the reasons people give for coming to the United States include seeking better job opportunities, joining family members already in the United States, furthering their education, and seeking political freedom (Furnham & Bochner, 1986, p. 46). The following table below illustrates how the number of African students has increased over the years.

Table 1
African international students in the United States from 1993-2008

School Year	Number of Students
1993-1994	20,569
1994-1995	20,724
1995-1996	20,844
1996-1997	22,078
1997-1998	23,162
1998-1999	26,222
1999-2000	30,292
2000-2001	34,217
2007-2008	35,654

In addition, foreign students contribute significant dollars to the U.S. economy. "In the 2002-2003 school year, the net contribution to the U.S. economy by foreign students was $12,851,000,000" (http://opendoorsiienetwork). Currently, that amount is up to $20, 000,000,000 (http://

opendoorsiienetwork). Due to this financial impact, educators and administrative personnel in higher education have developed support service programs, such as offices of international affairs or offices of international student services, to assist foreign students who have a variety of special needs to various factors encountered in their new cultural environments, such as the academic requirements of American institutions.

Delaware State University is indeed one of the many institutions of higher learning that admits international students. In 1996,127 foreign students were enrolled at Delaware State University (Delaware State University Fall 1998 Factbook). In 2000, 165 foreign students were enrolled at the university (Delaware State University Fall 2001 Factbook). There were 120 international students for the 2010-2011 school year, and twenty-one were from Africa (DSU International Students Office).

As a result of the many foreign students, Delaware State University is one of many institutions that have an office of international students set up to assist international students.

Problem at Hand

The general finding of the many studies on international students—such as those conducted by Cheng, 1999; Han, 1996; Lin & Yi, 1997; and Tseng, 2002—is that the major adjustment problems of international students involve financial and health concerns as well as living adjustments, which include, adjusting to American food and adapting to the climate. Other problems include academic issues, such as lack of proficiency in the English language and lack of understanding of the American educational system;

socio-cultural adaptation, such as culture shock, racial discrimination, and conflicts between American host standards (values and lifestyles) and those of home country; and psychological adjustment, which includes loneliness, depression, isolation, and loss of status and identity.

Like the international students at many universities, the African students at Delaware State University experienced a whole range of problems when they matriculated. These problems in one way or another impacted the way they adjusted and the speed with which they got acquainted to the American way of life. This study adopted a theoretical framework that focuses on the socio-cultural aspects of these experiences.

Importance of Study

Thousands of African students come to the United States every year to pursue a higher education, and these students face a variety of adjustment problems. In a study of the adjustment problems of African students at Michigan State University, Okafor (1986) stated that African students were found to have difficulties in getting used to American food and avoiding feelings of homesickness. He also concluded in his study that African students who have been in the United States for less than three years were found to have great difficulty in becoming acquainted with the U. S. system of education.

Dr. Blake's study, based on the fact that African students experience adjustment problems, sought to answer the following questions

1. What are the factors that cause adjustment problems for African students at Delaware State University?
2. How do the students cope (or deal) with such factors?
3. To what extent are the adjustment problems related to their length of stay in the United States?
4. How do African students at Delaware State University perceive the programs that the university has is place to help with their transition?
5. How do the African students describe their experiences at Delaware State University?

CHAPTER II

What the literature shows

This chapter is presented in three sections. The first section contains some theories and models of adjustment to help understand the adjustment processes of international students, the second presents studies that have been conducted on international students in general, and the third contains studies that have been conducted specifically on African students studying in the United States.

Theories and models of adjustment

Most international students in the United States are from cultures with close family ties and different patterns of etiquette, food habits, and religious beliefs. Since these students leave behind their families and social networks, they are forced to form new social networks in the United States. Cultural differences play a major role in international students' ability to form social relationships. International students often encounter personal, psychological, and social problems that directly affect their adjustment to a new culture. These combined experiences in many ways relate to what is commonly known as "culture shock."

"Culture shock" has been defined as a reaction to a new change in cultural environment. According to Oberg (1960) who coined the term, culture shock is "precipitated by the anxiety that results from losing all familiar signs and symbols of social intercourse" (p. 177). Church (1982) describes culture shock as "a normal process of adaptation to cultural stress, which involves symptoms such as anxiety, irritability and a longing for a more predictable environment" (qtd. in McKinlay, Pattison, & Gross, 1996, p. 379). Adler (1975) defines culture shock as "primarily a set of emotional reactions to the loss of perceptual reinforcements from one's own culture, to the new cultural stimuli which have little or no meaning, and to the understanding of new and diverse experiences" (p. 13). Winkelman (1994) defines "culture shock" as a multifaceted experience resulting from numerous stressors that occur when one makes contact with a different culture (p. 121). "The nature of culture shock experiences suggest that resolution can be addressed through cognitive orientation and behavioral adjustment involving recognition of cultural shock characteristics and implementation of strategies for its resolution" (Winkelman, 1994, p. 121). Moreover, he stated that there are many interrelated parts of cultural shock. These include emotional, interpersonal, cognitive, and social components, as well as the effects resulting from changes in socio-cultural relations, cognitive fatigue, role stress, and identity loss (p. 122).

Researchers have mentioned varying stages of cultural shock and its resolution. For example, Oberg's four stage model indicates that during the first stage of the adjustment process, visitors who go through culture shock are fascinated by the new environment, associate with people who speak their language, and are gracious to foreigners during their first few weeks of stay. The second stage is characterized by hostile and aggressive attitudes towards the host country. This attitude grows out of difficulty genuinely experienced by the visitor in his or her adjustment process. During the third stage, the visitor succeeds in understanding the language and begins to get acquainted with the new culture. Although the visitor may experience some level of difficulty adjusting, he or she takes a superior attitude to people of the host country and even makes jokes about adjustment experience. In the fourth stage, the visitor accepts the customs of the country as just another way of living and may operate within the new milieu without the feeling of anxiety, although there may be moments of strain in the adjustment process (pp. 178-179).

Adler (1975) mentions a five-stage transitional experience and adjustment process. These stages include contact, disintegration, reintegration, autonomy, and independence. These stages, he indicated, describe the transitional experiences of sojourners—those who move from one country to another country for a temporary stay.

Contact: According to Adler, in the initial contact with a second culture, the individual is still functionally integrated into his or her own culture. In the earliest contacts, the individual views the new environment from the insularity of his or her own ethnocentrism. The contact stage is marked by the excitement and euphoria of new experience. Similarities between the new culture and the individual's home culture tend to become validations of his or her own cultural status, role, and identity (p. 16).

Disintegration: The second stage is marked by a period of confusion and disorientation. Differences become increasingly noticeable as different behaviors, values, and attitudes intrude into the perceptual reality of the sojourner. More important is the growing sense of being different, isolated, and inadequate in the new situation (p. 16).

Reintegration: This stage is characterized by strong rejection of the second culture. In this stage of transition, the individual may regressively seek out relationships with only those of his or her own culture. The choice that the individual makes might depend on the intensity of the experiences, the general resiliency of the individual, or the interpretation and guidance provided by significant others (pp. 16-17).

Autonomy: marked by a rising sensitivity and by the acquisition of both skill and understanding of the second culture, sojourners at this stage are, to a large extent, independent of previous defensiveness and are experientially capable of moving in and out of new situations. An individual in this stage is relaxed and capable of verbally and nonverbally understanding other people, and is a fully functioning person (p. 17).

Independence: This final stage is marked by attitudes, emotionality, and behaviors that are independent but somehow influenced by cultural influence. The individual is capable of undergoing further transitions in life along new dimensions and of finding new ways to explore the diversity of human beings. Sojourners at this stage are humorous, creative, and are able to put meanings to situations (p. 18).

Rhinesmith (1985) presents an eight-stage intercultural adjustment cycle that includes application anxiety, selection/ arrival fascination, initial culture shock, surface adjustment, mental isolation, acceptance/integration, return anxiety, and reentry shock/reintegration. Below is Rhinesmith's explanation of his stages.

Application Anxiety: When waiting for an opportunity to go abroad, people experience anxiety over their chance of selection and their ability to handle their new opportunity. During this time, many anticipate cultural differences but have only a superficial awareness of potential adjustment problems (p. 152).

Selection/Arrival Fascination: When a person hears that he or she will be going abroad, the person experiences a rush of elation. During this stage, expectations for the visit are high and the pre-departure proceedings, as well as the arrival introductions, provide new stimuli and excitement about the potential of the new opportunity. On arrival, the person tends to be the focus of attention and activity (p. 152).

Initial Culture Shock: The initial fascination, along with the rounds of attention and parties, soon fades for someone who is remaining in a community over a period of time. Characteristics of this period include possible changes in sleeping patterns, excessive fatigue from speaking and listening to a foreign language, a lack of motivation to get up in the morning, and possible hostility toward some particular people or aspects of society (p. 152).

Surface adjustment: After this initial "down," which usually does not last more than a few days to a few weeks, a surface accommodation takes place between the visitor and his environment which allows that person to function at a relatively normal level without excellence. The person's language improves to the point where he can communicate basic ideas and feelings without fatigue, and learns how to make small groups of friends and associates (pp. 152-153).

Mental isolation: At some point, there is a desire for a deeper experience, greater language proficiency, and return to excellence in performance, which a sojourner many times experienced back home. At this point, the intractability of learning a new language proficiency is encountered, as are the inherent and often chronic weaknesses of the experience itself (p. 153).

Acceptance/integration: This stage is when the sojourner makes the important turnaround out of his mental isolation and decides to change the things that can be changed, and make the best of the rest. Eventually, the sojourner comes to accept his or her living situation and becomes more integrated into that surrounding (p. 153).

Return anxiety: Once settled in, the thought of leaving the new and familiar friends, faces, and community raises new anxieties similar to the experiences in stage one, before the departure. The sojourner begins to sense how much he or she has changed, and how much the new community has become a comfortable home for his or her new personality. The thought of returning to the old personality and back to old ways presents a threat and anxiety. The sojourner then fears that the people back home will not understand the new feelings and love that has been developed for the culture (p. 153).

Reentry shock/reintegration: The final resolution of this stage of adjustment involves an integration of overseas experience and culture, with one's new self-concept and with new realities of the back-home situation. This is a major life transition which, when successfully maneuvered, produces a new level of maturity and insight into oneself and the world. Once this is achieved, the sojourner will be able to turn to ways in which to become an active contribution in his or her "new" old life (p. 154).

Studies on international students

There are many reasons that administrators in colleges and universities welcome international students and scholars, and more authors have looked at international students studying in the United States more broadly. Selvadurai (1988) stated that these administrators "express a belief in the universal value of education and seek to further international understanding through the dissemination of knowledge" (p. 153). He also stated the following:

> Proponents of higher learning recognize that education is not only a means of permitting students to pursue academic and personal goals, but also an instrument in the economic, social, and political development of emerging countries. Hence, international students are considered a source of cultural diversity, enlightenment, and revenue [for institutions of higher learning]. (p. 153)

Despite the richness in cultural diversity that international students bring to American colleges, many studies indicate that these foreign students undergo many adjustment problems to make it through college successfully. In a study conducted in 1959, Santos identified six areas of adjustment that foreign students had to deal with. His findings revealed that the foreign students had to deal with personal problems, academic problems, religious concerns, emotional problems, social problems, and financial problems. Many of the students studied expressed difficulties in getting used to American food, and some felt lonely and were homesick.

According to Cheng (1999), Han (1996), Lin and Yi (1997) and Tseng (2002), these adjustment problems are academic, socio-cultural, psychological, and general living adjustment.

Common in the area of academic adjustment are the issues of lack of proficiency in the English language for some international students and a lack of understanding of the American system of education. Selvadurai (1998) revealed that the first barrier international students face is that of language. Many foreign students, he said, come from countries where English is not the first language. Although many of them are able to pass a standardized proficiency examination in English, they may have difficulty functioning satisfactorily in academic settings, and their difficulties in understanding lectures, expressing ideas, and writing reports have been attributed to their lack of proficiency in English (p. 154).

Mori (2000) echoed the sentiments of many researchers who have conducted studies on international students. Mori stated that language difficulties appear to be the most challenging issue for many international students. Lin and Yi (1997) indicated that it may be even more difficult for students who cannot express their academic abilities in English even though they may have had high academic achievement in their home countries.

"Recognizing that international students experience multiple adjustments within the campus culture, navigating the academic curriculum is a challenge" (Heggins & Jackson, 2003, p. 383). Because of the nature of the native culture of some foreign students, their classroom behaviors may be perceived as passive and shy (Heggins & Jackson, 2003, p. 384).

Many studies conducted on international students revealed that foreign students are likely to experience culture shock in the host countries. For example, Klineberg and Hull (1979) and Zwingman and Gunn (1983) found out that students are likely to face language difficulties, homesickness, and adjustment and psychological problems. Church (1982) stated that even though researchers agree that the problems foreign students face remain consistent, they differ in degree between different cultures.

The atmosphere in a classroom has also been reported by Craig (1981) to cause difficulty among international students. Most international students are trained to listen to the lecturers rather than speak in class, but the more open, collegial atmosphere maintained in U.S. classrooms may seem less formal for international students, thereby impeding their learning process.

Mori, 2000, and Sandhu & Asrabadi, 1994) have shown that international students tend to experience more problems than their American counterparts. These researchers have documented that international student populations have reported a variety of mental and personal concerns, including language barriers, academic difficulties, financial difficulties, interpersonal problems with American students, racial and ethnic discrimination, loss of social support, homesickness, and loneliness. Leon and Chou (1996) stated that the homesickness and culture shock experienced by international students in a foreign environment contribute to anxiety, confusion, insomnia, physical illness, and depression.

Studies on African students

Over the years, the number of African students enrolled in colleges and universities has been on the rise. Airen (1983) added the following:

> While significant statistical figures of foreign students from other continents (Asia, Europe, Latin and North America) could be found as representation of international learners in the United States in the early part of the century [20th century], only a handful of African students made it across the Atlantic Ocean. The turning point towards this realization actually gained momentum after many African nations obtained independence from their colonies. Since then, the increase continued on a pattern of growth. (p. 68)

Airen also stated that the short supply of colleges and universities in Africa is one of the reasons that African students continue to come to the United States for educational purposes (p. 68). In his study of the mental and social adaptation problems of African students at Pepperdine University, Airen found that adjustment problems in academic performances of the African students at the university did not to have any relationship with their communication skills and their perception of the Office of Foreign Students.

However, cultural change was proven to be significantly related to the attitudes of African students enrolled at the university in 1981.

Pruitt's (1978) study on the adaptation of African students on American campuses revealed that the difficulties African students faced were discrimination, depression, weather changes, homesickness, communication, and tiredness. He also states that the majority of them were satisfied with their educational experiences in the United States, while only a small number were comfortable with the American value system, dating practices, friendship and food.

In a study conducted by Essien (1975) on the interactions, perceptions, and attitudes of male Nigerian students toward the United States, the respondents indicated that they did not interact freely with Americans, even though they indicated that they interacted much more freely to the African Americans than white Americans.

Vukeh (1985) investigated the communication difficulties that West African students at the University of Minnesota encounter. In her findings, it was clear that the African students faced social and personal adjustment problems. Also, the students from French-speaking countries encountered more communication problems and adjustment problems than those from English speaking countries. Her findings also revealed that the African students went to the following for help in order of importance: first, students from their home country; then a faculty adviser; next, the international students advisers office; and finally, a counselor.

Nebedum-Ezeh, (1997) buttressed the findings of many researchers who have concluded that African students face adjustment problems in the United States. In his study of the experiences and coping strategies of African students at predominantly white institutions of higher learning, he found that African students experience adjustment difficulties upon arriving in the United States because of inadequate pre-departure orientation in their home countries and inadequate help when the arrive in the United States. African students' will to succeed often comes from self, family, friends, and the larger community where the African student is from. Coping strategies employed by these students include working harder to overcome academic problems and deficiencies, seeking help from African students and other foreign students, and seeking help from campus officials.

Another study that investigated the adjustment of African students was done at Michigan State University by Okafor (1986). As part of his findings, Okafor noted that although most of the African students did not experience very serious adjustment problems, many of them experienced very serious emotional, personal, and financial problems, while social, academic, and religious adjustments were the fewest problems. The most severe financial problems concern was finding jobs and having money for school expenses. In the area of personal and emotional problems, the African students at Michigan State University had difficulties getting used to American foods, and they felt homesick. He also concluded that African students who perceived the orientation programs they received as inadequate experienced greater difficulty than those who perceived the program as somewhat helpful or very helpful in getting used to American food, being accepted in social groups, and participating freely in extracurricular activities.

Ekaiko (1981) investigated the effects of selected cultural and environmental factors on the social and academic adjustment of African students at Michigan universities. In his findings, he concluded that communication, as a variable, seems to affect the adjustment of African students.

He found out that the more effective African students are in communicating with Americans, the more effective they are with schoolwork. While he found out that climate, as a variable, did not seem to affect the Africans' academic and social adjustment, communication and climate combined seemed to affect either the social or their academic adjustment. Ekaiko also stated that the pattern of social adjustment of the African students was that they associated more with their fellow countrymen, other Africans, and other foreign students.

None of the above mentioned studies have been conducted at a historically black college or university. My study will contribute a unique perspective to this literature in that it will focus on how African students, primarily blacks, adjust to another primarily black institution in the United States and how they perceive both the services the institution offers to help them adjust and their experiences at the university.

Brief history of Delaware State University

Delaware State University, formally known as the State College for Colored Students, was established in 1891 by the Delaware General Assembly under the provisions of the Second Morrill Act of 1890. This Act provided a permanent annual endowment for each land-grant college established under the provision of the Morrill Act of 1862, and it also allowed a portion of the federal appropriation to be used for the endowment, support, and maintenance of land-grant colleges. Delaware State University is the only Historically Black College and University (HBCU) in the state of Delaware. Over the years, Delaware State University has grown into a 400-acre institution with many buildings and a walk-in campus. It currently serves approximately 5,000 students, including Delawareans, students from around the country, and students from around the world. Its main campus is in Dover, with satellite campuses in Georgetown and New Castle. Its mission is outlined below:

> Delaware State University is a public, comprehensive, 1890 land-grant institution that offers access and opportunity to diverse populations from Delaware, the nation, and the world. Building on its heritage as a historically black college, the University purposefully integrates the highest standards of excellence in teaching, research, and service in its baccalaureate, master's and doctoral programs. Its commitment to advance science, technology, liberal arts, and the professions produces capable and productive leaders who contribute to the sustainability and economic development of the global community. www. (Desu.edu)

CHAPTER III

Ways the data were collected
and treated

This methods section provides details on this study's participants, design and instrumentation, and the treatment of data. Data were collected using a survey questionnaire, two focus groups, and observation. These methods of collecting data were chosen for three reasons. First, a review of the literature on this topic revealed that surveys and focus groups were the two data collection methods most often used. The observation method I chose to do since I could easily observe the participants in my place of study. Secondly, given the time frame for this study, analyzing data from these methods was the most expedient way to conduct the study. Finally, the three methods will serve as a triangulation of my data collection methods. Denzin (1970) states that triangulation is when one collects information from a diverse range of individuals and settings, using a variety of methods (qtd. in Maxwell, 1996, p. 75). "Triangulation reduces the risk that your conclusions will reflect only the systematic biases or limitations of a specific method, and it allows you to gain a better assessment of the validity and generality of the explanations that you develop" (Maxwell, 1996, pp. 75-76).

Participants

Many researchers, such as Arubi (1979), Khimulu (1981) and Sanders (1969) agreed that foreign students in the United States go through some adjustment problems, irrespective of their countries of origin. The purpose of this study was to investigate the experiences and adjustment problems of one segment of foreign students studying in the United States-African students enrolled at Delaware State University.

Participants for this study were 57 African students who were enrolled at Delaware State University. The African students, whose names were retrieved from the Admissions Office, were from nine countries in Africa.

Instruments and Design

The instrument used in this study was a survey questionnaire; focus groups and observations were also used to gather data. The 30-question survey was a modification of Santos's (1959) Foreign Student Problem Checklist and Okafor's (1986) survey. The first part of the survey consisted of 11 questions that requested geographic and background information on the participants. The second section contained a checklist of the students' experiences, adjustment problems, and perception of Delaware State University. Attached to the survey were a cover letter addressed to the participants and a research consent form.

All the participants were first contacted either in person or on the phone about the form, purposes, and reason for of this study. Sixty-two of the surveys were hand-delivered by me to the participants. Five of the surveys, however, were mailed because the participants lived out of town and could not be contacted in person. My reason for choosing the hand-delivery and pick-up method was because, as Babbie (1973) stated, it yields a high return rate and it reduces cost.

Focus groups

Two sets of focus groups (seven students in each group: three graduate students and 11 undergraduate students) were also used to gather information for this study. Krueger (1994) and Morgan (1988) stated that gathering information using focus groups is advantageous when the interaction among the interviewees will yield the best information and when one-on-one interviews may yield hesitant information. The 14 students were asked 12 questions ranging from their experiences to their adjustment problems at Delaware State University, and how they dealt with such problems. These questions solicited answers that illuminated the students' experiences, the problems they face, how they cope with such problems, and their perceptions of Delaware State University. The students for these focus groups were selected through a systematic random process. The focus group sessions, which met for about one hour each, were taped, and students had to sign a consent form to participate. The data collected were transcribed, and some of the text information was used alongside the analysis of the survey responses. The focus group questions were drawn primarily from the survey questions.

Observations

The third method used for this study was observation. Maxwell (1996) stated that, "Observation often enables you to draw inferences about someone's meaning and perspective that you couldn't obtain by relying exclusively on interview data"

(p. 76). I kept a journal of the observations I made through conversations I had with the African students at Delaware State University. The conversations I had with them, even though they may include other things, involved their experiences and how they were adjusting (the students had no idea what my intentions were). After such conversations, I noted relevant information that helped me understood why they responded in certain ways on their surveys. The observation piece of my study provided examples to substantiate the findings from my survey and focus groups.

Treatment of Data

The data collected from the survey were transferred to Microsoft Excel and then analyzed using statistical tests. Since the survey instrument yielded non-parametric data, it was appropriate to use simple statistical technique. Thus, Chi-square tests were used to examine the relationship between respondents' background characteristics and the degree of difficulty they face. Descriptive statistics of mean, percentages, and standard deviation were used to analyze the adjustment problems. The focus group interviews were transcribed and analyzed. The journal entries, which were kept to understand some of the responses on the survey form, were also analyzed and discussed. The next chapter (Chapter IV) presents an analysis of the data.

CHAPTER IV

The results

This chapter presents data analysis of the survey, supplemented by focus group interviews and journal entry. From the returned questionnaire and their subsequent coded data, the first part of this chapter contains descriptive statistics of the respondents' background information from the survey, while the second part examines the relationship between respondents' background and the degree of adjustment problems they face.

Characteristics and background of participants

Sixty-seven of the 69 African students enrolled at Delaware State University in the mid 2000s were handed surveys for this study. There were a total of 57 responses (85.1%) out of the 67 surveys that were distributed. Two responses were received out of the five surveys mailed, and responses were received for 55 out of the 62 surveys that were hand delivered. Of the 57 respondents, 54.4% were males and 45.6% were females. Seventy-four percent of the respondents were 27 years of age or younger, while 26% were 28 years of age or older.

Table 2 Age of respondents

Count	Cum. Count	Percent	Cum. percent	Age
25	25	43.9	43.9	18-22
18	43	31.6	75.4	23-27
7	50	12.3	87.7	28-32
2	52	3.5	91.2	33-37
5	57	8.8	100	38 and older

In terms of the respondents' nationalities, the majority of them are from West African countries, where the British and American systems of education are used and English is the official language of instruction. As to the participants' educational level, 17.5% were freshmen, 26.3% were sophomores, 17.5% were juniors, 15.8% were seniors, and 22.8% were graduate students.

Table 3
Respondents' nationality and background on their system of education

Count	Cum. Count	Percent	Cum. Percent	country	System of education
10	10	17.5	17.5	Cameroon	British
16	26	28.1	45.6	Ghana	British
1	27	1.8	47.4	Ivory Coast	French
2	29	3.5	50.9	Kenya	British
5	34	8.8	59.6	Liberia	American

19	53	33.3	93.0	Nigeria	British
1	54	1.8	94.7	Somalia	Somalian
1	55	1.8	96.5	Tanzania	British
2	57	3.5	100	Uganda	British

For the participants' responses as to whether or not they went through a formal orientation about the American system of education, 21.1% indicated yes, while 78.9% said no; but 24.6% said they had an orientation about the American culture, while 75.4% said they did not.

Regarding the financing of their education, 14% indicated that they received funds solely from Delaware State University, 40% state that family members and relatives pay for their education, 17.5% indicated the U.S. government pays their tuition, 12.3% said they pay their own tuition, 3.5% (excluding the 14% that receive funds from DSU) state that they receive money from Delaware State University to supplement funds from their relatives, 8.8% responded that they receive money from the U.S. government and their family, and 3.5% fund their own tuition with the help of the U.S. government. The analysis showed that the majority of foreign students fund their own education themselves, and usually with the help of family members and relatives.

As to the participants' length of stay in the United States, 1.8% of the respondents indicated they have been here for three to six months, 3.5% have been in the United States for six months to one year, 14% have been in the United States for one to two years, 14% have been in the United States for two to three years, 17.5% have been in the United States for three to four years, and 49.1% have been in the United States for four years or more.

Adjustment problems as outlined in the survey

A total of 14 adjustment problems were the focus of this study. Table 4 shows the percentage distribution of responses in percentages for each problem. Each adjustment problem was coded 0, 1, 2, and 3. The 0 represented not a problem, the 1 represented somewhat of a problem, the 2 represented problem, and the 3 represented serious problem. Each adjustment problem is numbered as it appears in the questionnaire.

Table 4
Distribution of percentages according to adjustment problems

Item number and name	Not a problem (%)	Somewhat of a problem (%)	Problem (%)	Serious problem (%)	Cumulative Problem (%)
1. understanding the English language	82.5	17.5			17.5
2. familiarity with U. S. customs	47.0	42.0	11.0		53.0
3. getting acquainted with the U.S. system of education	68.4	26.3	5.3		31.6
4. getting academic advisement	58.0	26.0	16.0		42.0
5. understanding instructors	77.0	18.0	5.0		23.0

6. experiencing racial and ethnic discrimination	38.5	30.0	24.5	7.0	61.5
7. financing education	28.0	40.4	19.3	12.3	72.0
8. feeling homesick	24.6	47.4	14.0	14.0	75.4
9. feeling lonely	53.0	31.5	12.0	3.5	47.0
10. immigration limitations	42.0	16.0	14.0	28.0	58.0
11. funding healthcare services	40.0	26.0	16.0	18.0	60.0
12. getting used to U.S. foods	52.6	29.8	10.6	7.0	47.4
13. making American friends	58.0	26.2	10.5	5.3	42.0
14. making friends with other international students	79.0	16.0	2.0	3.0	21.0
Total	53.5	28.1	11.4	7.0	50.8

Research question 1

While the majority of respondents indicated that they did not have to face adjustment problems, it is clear that many of them had to deal with adjustment problems in varying degrees. Of the 46.5%, who experienced adjustment problems, 7% of the respondents had serious problems. Table 4 shows that the majority of students had to deal with adjustment problems in the areas of immigration limitations, feeling homesick, financing education, familiarity with U. S. customs, funding healthcare services, and experiencing racial and ethnic discrimination. Issues that were not problems for the majority of African students were understanding the English language, understanding instructors, making friends with Americans and other international students, getting acquainted with the U.S. system of education, and getting academic advisement.

Focus group discussions and journal entries support the claim that the students did not have problems with the English language because they came from countries where English is the official language. Focus group discussions and journal entries also support the claim that they face discrimination because they are stereotyped as coming from low-life backgrounds and because of their accents. The students indicated that paying their tuition is a big burden on them and their families because, as students (those who are on student visas), they are not allowed to work in the United States, and it is difficult for their relatives to pay for their education from the income they get in their respective countries.

Research question 2

Responses from the focus group discussions revealed that African students coped with the adjustment problems they faced in two ways. First, they stated that they found themselves studying and working harder to overcome academic and social problems because they sometimes experience subtle discrimination practices from some of their colleagues and some instructors. As one student puts it, "When I speak in class, some of the other students laugh at my accent." As a result, I just keep to myself, even though I may have something to say." These experiences, they stated, are mainly stereotypical in nature. Second, the African students indicated that they also cope with the adjustment problems they face by forming a social support among other African students and other international students, who may be experiencing the same adjustment problems. Another student stated, "It is not that we want to just stay with other Africans, we feel more comfortable when we are with one another."

Table 5 shows the number count and percentages of the responses to the participants who had orientation on either the American system of education and/or the American culture.

Table 5
Orientation on American culture and education

Respondents	Number count	Percentage count	Orientation not helpful (%)	Orientation helpful (%)
Respondents who did not receive orientation	38	67.0	N/A	N/A
Respondents who received orientation	19	33.0	3.5	29.5
Total	57	100	3.5	29.5

The focus group interviews revealed that many of the African students did not have to go through an orientation about the university and the United States because of the time constraints they had from the time they got accepted at Delaware State University to the time they arrived in the United States, even though the university offers an orientation program.

Responses for students' use of the counseling office indicated that 80% of the African students do not use the counseling service, 18.5% use it sometimes, and 1.5% use it all the time. The focus group interviews revealed that many of the students do not know of the counseling office, and a good number of them consider some of their problems personal and do not want to share it with other people. All the students who use the counseling office agree that it was helpful to them.

Research question 3

Regarding the respondents' length of stay and if that has an effect on their adjustment problems, 56% stated that the problems they face have nothing to do with their length of stay, while 44% indicated that their length of stay has an effect on the problems that they faced. The problems many of them face, they said, they will continue to face because of things like their immigration status, their accents, and issues relating to the differences in the culture they grew up in and the U.S. culture.

Research question 4

The majority of the students indicated that the services offered by the International Students Office were inadequate for several reasons. Journal entries and focus group interviews reveal that the students are disappointed most when they have to vacate the school premises for short holidays, such as Thanksgiving and Easter when many of them do not have relatives in the state of Delaware or even in the United States for that matter. They believed that the office, in particular and the university as a whole, should provide housing for them. The students also stated that they want to get a sense of belonging to the university. Although there is an international student body, they stated; For the most part they are left on their own. They want to see the International Students Office play a bigger role in their adjustment process, hold regular meetings with the foreign students and sponsor extracurricular activities.

Table 6
Respondents' perceptions of the services offered by Delaware State University's International Students Office to help African students adjust

Respondents	Number Count	Inadequate services (%)	Adequate services (%)
Respondents who state services are inadequate	37	65.0	-
Respondents who state services are adequate	20	-	35.0
Total	57	65.0	35.0

Research question 5

An overwhelming majority of African students at Delaware State University responded that their experiences at the university are good. They attributed this to the high level of instruction and the fact that the student body and faculty and staff are diverse. Some of those who stated that they have not had good experiences cited problems with the administration over payment of tuition, while others cited discrimination and stereotyping from instructors.

Table 7
Respondents' experiences at Delaware State University

Respondents	Number count	Good experience (%)	Not a good experience (%)
Respondents with good experience	51	89.5	
Respondents without a good experience	6		10.5
Total	57	89.5	10.5

Tests of relationships

This section presents information on whether or not there is a relationship between some background characteristics and some of the adjustment problems outlined in this study. Chi-square tests were used to show the relationships, and the significant levels for these tests were set at 0.05.

Table 8

Test of relationship between respondents' classification
and problems financing their education

Financing education	Freshmen and sophomores (%)	Juniors and seniors (%)	Graduate students (%)	Total (%)	Number count
Not a problem	5.263	15.789	7.018	28.070	16
Problem	38.596	17.544	15.789	71.930	41
Total	43.860	33.333	22.807	100.000	
Number count	25	19	13		57

Test statistic	Value	Df	Prob
Pearson Chi-square	6.749	2.000	0.034

The result of the test of relationship between students' classification and problems financing their education revealed that there is a significant relationship between the two. Undergraduate students have more difficulty financing their education than graduate students. This is so because some graduate students are able to get assistantships and scholarships for their education. While this may seem obvious to some readers, it is not easy for foreign students to get assistantship. The result also showed that undergraduates in their first two years of college have greater difficulty in paying for their tuition than their last two years. This is so for foreign students because they are usually not allowed to work their first year of college because of immigration issues. And in many cases, it takes these students two years to get accustomed to the American system for them to acquire jobs on campus or out of campus to help finance their education.

Table 9
Test of relationship between respondents' classification and problem experiencing discrimination

Experiencing racial and ethnic discrimination	Freshmen and sophomores (%)	Juniors and seniors (%)	Graduate students (%)	Total (%)	Number count
Not a problem	14.035	14.035	10.526	38.596	22
Problem	29.825	19.298	12.281	61.404	35
Total	43.860	33.333	22.807	100.000	
Number count	25	19	13		57

Test statistic	Value	Df	Prob
Pearson Chi-square	0.871	2.000	0.647

The result of the test of relationship between respondents' classification and experience with racial and ethnic discrimination revealed that there is no significant relationship between the two. However, undergraduate students indicated that they experienced more racial and ethnic discrimination than graduate students, and African undergraduate students experience the most discrimination during their first two years of college.

Table 10

Test of relationship between respondents' gender and problems experiencing racial and ethnic discrimination

Experiencing racial and ethnic discrimination	Males (%)	Female (%)	Total (%)	Number count
Not a problem	22.807	15.789	38.596	22
Problem	31.579	29.825	61.404	35
Total	54.386	45.614	100.000	
Number count	31	26		57

Test statistic	Value	df	Prob
Pearson Chi-square	0.32	1.000	0.572

The findings of the test of relationship between respondents' gender and problems experiencing racial and ethnic discrimination indicated that there is no significant relationship between the two. While the majority of African students indicated that they experience discrimination, many of them said that they do not. The majority of men also stated that they experience more racial and ethnic discrimination than women.

Table 11

Test of relationship between respondents' classification and how they rated the services Delaware State University has in place to help them adjust

Services	Freshmen and Sophomores (%)	Juniors and seniors (%)	Graduate students (%)	Total (%)	Number count
Not adequate	29.825 (%)	17.544	17.544	64.912	37
Adequate	14.035	15.789	5.263	35.088	20
Total	43.860	33.333	22.807	100.000	
Number count	25	19	13		57

Test statistic	Value	Df	Prob
Pearson Chi-square	2.186	2.000	0.335

Although the result of the test of relationship between respondents' classification and how they rated the services that the university has in place to help them adjust yielded no significant relationship, it was clear that the majority of the students stated that the services were not adequate. Undergraduate students in their first two years felt that the services were inadequate the most. These undergraduate students in their first two years felt this way the most because that is when they are new to the U.S. college environment and have to adjust to the new system.

Table 12
Test of relationship between respondents' classification and their familiarity with U.S. customs

Familiarity with customs	Freshmen and sophomores (%)	Juniors and seniors (%)	Graduate students (%)	Total	Number count
Not a problem	15.789	21.053	10.526	47.368	27
Problem	28.070	12.281	12.281	52.632	30
Total	43.860	33.333	22.807	100.000	
Number count	25	19	13		57

Test statistic	Value	df	Prob
Pearson Chi-square	3.204	2.000	0.202

The result of the test of relationship between respondents' classification and familiarity with U.S. customs revealed that there is no significant relationship between the two. Although the majority of African students saw this as a problem, students in their first two years of college stated that their unfamiliarity with U.S. customs was more of a problem than upperclassmen and graduate students. Again, because these students are relatively new to the environment, they had to adjust to too many things.

Table 13
Test of relationship between respondents' gender and feeling homesick

Feeling homesick	Male (%)	Female (%)	Total (%)	Number count
Not a problem	8.772	15.789	24.561	14
Problem	45.614	29.825	75.439	43
Total	54.386	45.614	100.000	
Number count	31	26		57

Test statistic	Value	df	Prob
Pearson Chi-square	2.608	1.000	0.106

The result of the test of relationship between gender and feeling homesick showed that there is no significant relationship between the two. The majority of the respondents indicated that they felt homesick. In many cases, these students had left their loved ones and friends in their homelands and were pursuing degrees in a different country. The majority of males felt more homesick than the females.

Table 14
Test of relationship between respondents' gender and experience at Delaware State University

Experience at DSU	Male (%)	Female (%)	Total (%)	Number count
Not good	7.018	3.509	10.526	6
Good	47.368	42.105	89.474	51
Total	54.386	45.614	100.000	
Number count	31	26		57

Test statistic	Value	df	Prob
Pearson Chi-square	0.408	1.000	0.523

While the result of the test of relationship between respondents' gender and their experiences at Delaware State University showed no significant relationship, an overwhelming majority indicated that their experiences are good. The majority of Males felt that their experiences were good more than the females.

CHAPTER V

Conclusions and
recommendations

Restatement of Purpose

This study was designed to investigate the experiences and adjustment problems of African students enrolled in the spring semester of 2004 at Delaware State University. In order for constructive measures to be taken to minimize the adjustment problems of these students and prospective African students, this study specifically looked at the factors that cause the adjustment problems of African students enrolled at Delaware State University, the strategies that these students use to cope with such problems, the extent to which the adjustment problems are related to their length of stay in the United States, and how they perceive the programs that he university has in place to help with their adjustment.

Restatement of research questions

Thousands of African students are admitted to many institutions of higher learning in the United States every year, and as many researchers in this area have concluded (Vukeh,1985; Okafor, 1996; and Cheng, 1999, for example), these students have to deal with adjustment problems in varying degrees.

The African students at Delaware State University are no exceptions to many of the adjustment problems faced by international students in general. This study attempted to answer the following questions:

1. What are the factors that cause adjustment problems for African students at Delaware State University?
2. How do the students cope (or deal) with such factors?
3. To what extent are the adjustment problems related to their length of stay in the United States?
4. How do African students at Delaware State University perceive the programs that the university has is place to help with their transition?
5. How do the African students describe their experiences at Delaware State University?

Procedures employed in the study

This descriptive study was conducted by the use of three procedures. First, a modified version of Santos's 1959 adjustment problem checklist and Okafor's (1986) questionnaire was used to gather data. The survey was pilot-tested for congruency. Sixty-seven of the 69 African students enrolled in the spring semester of 2004 at Delaware State University received a copy of the questionnaire. Ninety-three percent of the questionnaire was hand-delivered, and 7% was mailed because of the distant location of the prospective participants. Second, a systematic random sampling was used to select two focus groups that were also used to collect data; and third, an observation method was also used to gather data.

Summary of findings

Based on the 57 participants from the nine countries included in this study, the findings were as follows:

Answer to research question 1

The factors that caused adjustment problems for African students enrolled at Delaware State University are immigration limitations, feeling homesick, financing education, familsiarity with U.S. customs, funding healthcare, and racial and ethnic discrimination.

Answer to research question 2

The African students indicated that they cope with the adjustment problems they faced in two ways. First, they worked harder to overcome academic and social problems;

second, they formed social support networks among other African students and other international students because, for the most part, they feel much more comfortable among those students.

Answer to research question 3

While some students indicated that the adjustment problems they faced was related to their length of stay, the majority of students indicated that the problems they faced had nothing to do with the adjustment problems they faced. Some of them believed that no matter how long they stay in the United States, they will continue to experience the same problems.

Answer to research question 4

The majority of African students stated that Delaware State University did not have adequate services to help them with their adjustment. They believed that for the most part, they were left to fend for themselves after they went through the process of registering for classes.

Answer to research question 5

An overwhelming majority of the African students at Delaware State University indicated that they had good experiences at

Delaware State University. They attributed
their good experiences to the diversity of the
institution.

Additional findings

1. In general, although the majority of African
   students did not experience adjustment problems,
   there were many others who did and a few who
   experienced serious adjustment problems. The
   students had the least problem understanding
   the English language, since the majority of them
   are from English speaking countries.
2. The African undergraduate students had more
   difficulty financing their education than graduate
   students.
3. While the majority of African students
   indicated that they experienced racial and ethnic
   discrimination, the most of males stated that they
   experience more discrimination than females.
4. Although the majority of African students stated
   that the services offered by Delaware State
   University to help them adjust were inadequate,
   the students in their first two years felt the services
   were inadequate than upperclassmen students
   and graduate students.
5. The majority of African students noted that
   familiarity with U.S. customs was a problem.
   However, freshmen and sophomores indicated
   that this was more of a problem for them than
   juniors, seniors, and graduate students.
6. In the area of feeling homesick, the majority
   of African students indicated that they felt

homesick. They stated that they missed their family members and loved once back home. The males felt more homesick than the females.

7. In general, an overwhelming majority of the African students stated that they had good experiences at Delaware State University. More males than female felt that they had good experiences.

8. The majority of African students at Delaware State University funded their own education, with the help and support of their families and relatives

9. An overwhelming majority of the African students did not use the counseling services at Delaware State University because of two reasons. First, some of them were not aware that the services existed; second, those who knew of the services chose not to use it because they wanted to keep their problems private.

10. When it came to orientation, most of the African students did not go through any formal orientation because of time constraints regarding their travel to the United States.

11. In general, the majority of African students did not have problems making friends with Americans and other international students.

12. While many African students at Delaware State University had problems getting used to U.S. foods, the majority of them did not.

13. The African students indicated that they did not have problems understanding instructors.

14. Even though the majority of African students indicated that they did not have problems getting

academic advisement, many of them stated that they had problems in this area.

15. The demographic data showed that the majority of African students during the spring of 2004 were from West Africa, and there were more African males than African females.

16. Most of the African students indicated that they were not lonely.

17. Based on the focus group discussion, many of the African students indicated that the weather was a problem for them. They are not used to the extreme cold weather in the winter and the hot weather in the summer.

Discussions and implications of the study

The analyses of the data for this study collected from the questionnaire, focus groups, and observations provided information on the experiences and adjustment problems of African students at Delaware State University. Many of the problems enumerated on are common among foreign students in the United States. The recommendations from studies such as this one will not eliminate such problems, but they will limit or curb the degree at which many of these students experience these problems. This study, in many ways, supports the research models that were mentioned.

Although some of the findings are similar to many studies conducted on African students enrolled at U.S. college campuses, such as African students having problems with immigration, feeling homesick, and experiencing racial and ethnic discrimination, it did not reveal the same findings in the areas of problems with the English language, understanding instructors, and getting acquainted with the

U.S. system of education. This study, which is indeed a groundbreaking one on any aspect of international students at Delaware State University, will open the doors for further research on foreign students and their impact on the university.

It is my hope that the administration will design programs and policies based on the findings and suggestions of this study.

Limitations of the study

This study was limited because participants were only African students enrolled at Delaware State University. Another possible limitation to this study is the fact that some specific data were not available from the International Students Office (for example, the name of the first foreign student and year-by-year statistics since the first student was admitted). Also, this study focused not just on African students who are enrolled as foreign students, but all students who hold African citizenship. Finally, the following conclusions were drawn based on the findings of this study. Although some of these findings can reflect adjustment problems experienced by African students in other college campuses, these findings specifically reflect the problems experienced by African students at Delaware State University. Thus, these findings are not generalizable to all African students in all U.S. College campuses.

Recommendations

Based on the findings of this study, the following are recommendations for program implementation:

1. Delaware State University should implement a program wherein foreign students can help manage an office of international students' affairs, similar to the Student Government Association. Students who manage this office can be the official voice of the international students.

2. Since many African students experienced immigration problems, which is usually the case with foreign students because of their limited immigration status, Delaware State University can implement a program that gives financial aid and assistantships (such as a work-study program) to students who excel academically. This will help reduce the financial burden on the African students in particular and the international students as a whole, since many of these students cannot work.

3. The implementation of a mentor program for the African students will help curb some of the problems that they faced. Since there are many African professors at Delaware State University, such a mentor program will serve as a social support and help students with their adjustment problems.

4. African students should form an African Students Organization under the umbrella body of the International Students Association. This will also help African students come together and form social support networks.

Based on the findings of this study, the following are recommendations for policy implementation:

1. Delaware State University should implement a more comprehensive orientation program that addresses the campus life of the institution and the American culture and education system for all foreign students who are accepted to the university. Normally, orientation sessions are usually held only before the start of classes. This policy will make provisions for students who are not on campus for orientation before the start of classes to be able to go through an orientation process.

2. Given the fact that some African students are enrolled at Delaware State University with no immediate relatives in Delaware and neighboring states, the university should adopt a policy whereby African students in particular and international students in general do not have to leave the campus on short holidays, such as Easter and Thanksgiving since they do not have a place to stay.

3. It is strongly recommended that a comprehensive (regularly updated) database of African students in particular and international students in general be kept so that members of the faculty, staff, and students of Delaware State University and others who want to conduct research on these students can readily have access to it.

4. It is also strongly recommended that Delaware State University consistently publish data on African students and international students in its Students' Profile section of its yearly factbook.

5. Counselors who meet with international students should be prepared and trained to discuss issues related to international students.
6. International students' files should be kept separately from in-state and out-of-state students' files.

Recommendations for further research

1. Since it is apparent that the majority of the African students do not think that Delaware State University provides enough services for the students, further research into other problems that these students face may lead to more program and policy implementation.
2. It is recommended that a comparative study be done on the adjustment problems of African students and other international students at Delaware State University.
3. It is also recommended that a study be conducted on the perception of the faculty on African students at Delaware State University.
4. A comparative study should be done on the adjustment problems of African students at Delaware State University and another historically black college.

What the educational experiences of African students in America mean to us

Final Thoughts

The United States of America is what it is: the most powerful nation in the world. While the ideologies of citizens from other countries may vary, the African students agree that there is no country that comes close to the United States based on its opportunities for all of its citizens. The experiences and adjustment problems the Africans experienced opened their eyes to what many other countries can look like. There are educational opportunities, political opportunities, economical opportunities, and many other opportunities that are available to everyone. Many of the African students, though they came with the intentions of going back after their studies, decided to stay in the United States and work because they can earn enough money to take care of their families.

To all of the African students, coming here was a blessing, and no other experiences could be compared to this. Even amid their frustrations, their experiences have revealed that getting educated in America has taught them to be resolved in whatever they do and that was the best thing that could have happened to them.

REFERENCES

Adler, P. (1975). The traditional experience: An alternative view of cultural shock. *Journal of Humanistic Psychology*, *15*, 13-23.

Airen, P. I. (1983). An investigation into the mental and social adaptation problems of African students at Pepperdine University. Doctoral dissertation. Pepperdine University

Arubi, E. A. (1979) A comparative analysis of identified problems as perceived by Nigerian students enrolled in the regents system in Kansas. Unpublished doctoral dissertation, Kansas State University.

Babbie, E. R. (1973). Survey research Methods. Belmont, CA. Wadsworth

Cheng, E. H. (1999). A study of international students' adjustment problems at the University of South Dakota. Unpublished doctoral dissertation, University of Dakota.

Church, A. T. (1982). Sojourner Adjustment. *Psychological Bulletin*, *91*, 540-572

Delaware State University Fall 1998 Factbook.

Delaware State University Fall 2001 Factbook.

Denzin, N. K. (1970) Sociological methods: a sourcebook. Chicago, Aldine Publication Company.

Ekaiko, U. T. O. (1981). The effects of selected cultural and environmental factors on the social and academic adjustment of African students in United States Universities. Doctoral dissertation. Wayne State University.

Essien, I. M. (1975). An investigation of the interaction, perception, and attitudes of male Nigerian students toward the United States. Unpublished doctoral dissertation, Kansas State University.

Furnham, A. & Bochner, S. (1986). Culture Shock: Psychological reactions to unfamiliar environment. Methuen: New york

Hagey, A. R. & Hagey, J. (1974). Meeting the needs of students from other cultures. *Improving College and University Teaching, 22*, 42-44.

Han, H. Y. (1996). A study of adjustment problems of Korean students in the Pittsburgh area. Unpublished doctoral dissertation, University of Pittsburgh.

Hayes, R. L., & Lin, H. R. (1994). Coming to America: developing social support systems for international students. *Journal of Multicultural Counseling and Development, 22*, 7-16

Heggins III, W. & Jackson, J. (2003). Understanding the collegiate experience for Asian international students at a Midwestern research university. *College Student Journal, 37*(3), 379-392.

Http://opendoorsiienetwork. Information retrieved March 31, 2004.

Institute of International Education (2011). Foreign student and total U.S. enrollment. Information retrieved November 24, 2011 from http://www.opendoorsweb.org

Institute of International Education (2001). Foreign student and total U.S. enrollment. Information retrieved December 2, 2003 from http://www.opendoorsweb.org/2001%20files/layout.html.

Khimulu, M. M. (1981) The adjustment of East African students pursuing academic programmes in California. Doctoral dissertation. United States International University.

Klineberg, O. & Hull, W. F. (1979). At a foreign university: An international study of adaptation and coping. New York: Praeger

Krueger, R. A. (1994). Focus groups: A practical guide for applied research (2nd. Ed.). Thousand Oaks, CA

Leong, F. T. L. & Chou, E. L. (1996). Counseling international students. In P. B. Penderson; J.G. Draguns; W.J. Lonner; & J. T. Trimble (Eds.), Counseling across cultures (4th ed., pp. 210-242). Thousand Oaks, CA.

Lin, J. C. & Yi, J. K. (1997). Asian international students' adjustment: Issues and program suggestions. *College Student Journal, 31*(4), 473-479.

Mallinckrodt, B. & Leong, F. T. L. (1992). International graduate students, stress, and social support. *Journal of college Student Development, 33*, 71-78.

Maxwell, J. A. (1996) Qualitative research design: An interactive approach. Thousand Oaks, CA.

McKinlay, N. J., Pattison, H. M. & Gross, H. (1996). An exploratory investigation of the effects of a cultural orientation programme on the psychological well-being of international university students. *Higher Education, 31*(3), 379-395.

Mori, S. (2000). Addressing the mental health concerns of international students. *Journal of Counseling and Development, 78*, 137-144.

Morgan, D. L. (1988). Focus groups as qualitative research. Newbury Park, CA.

National Center for Educational Statistics

Nebedum-Ekeh, G. C. (1997). An examination of the experiences and coping strategies of African students at predominantly white institutions of higher education in the United States. Doctoral dissertation. University of Massachusetts Amherst.

Oberg, K. (1954). Culture shock. Indianapolis, IN: Bobbs-Merril.

Oberg, K. (1960). *Cultural shock: adjustment to new cultural environments. Practical Anthropology, 7,* 177-182.

Okafor, C. (1986). Adjustment of African students at Michigan State University. Doctoral dissertation. Michigan State University. Dissertation Abstracts International, 47, 07

Pruitt, F. J. (1978). The adaptation of African students to American society. *International Journal of Intercultural Relations. 2*(1), 90-116

Rhinesmith, S. (1985). Bring home the world. New York: Walker & Co.

Sanders, I. T. (Ed.). (1961). The professional education from other lands. New York: Council on Social Work Education.

Sandhu, D. S. & Asrabadi, B. R. (1994). Development of an acculturative stress scale for international students: primary findings. *Psychological Reports, 75,* 435-448.

Santos, A. (1959). A study of the problems faced by foreign students at Indiana

University. Indiana: Indiana University. Condensed from Cross Cultural Education. Dissertation by Franklin T. Burroughs, University of Southern California Los Angeles, 1964.

Selvadurai, R. (1998). Problems faced by international students in American colleges and universities. *Community Review, 16,* 153-159

Schlossberg, N. K., Waters, E. B., & Goodman, J. (1995). *Counseling adults in transition* (2nd ed.). New York: Springer.

Stafford, T. H. (1980). Adjustment of international students. *NASPA Journal,* 18(1), 40-45

Tseng, Wen-Chih. International students' strategies for well-being. *College Student Journal, 36*(4), 591-597.

Vukeh, E. N. (1985). Communication problems of West African students at the University of Minnesota (oral, academic, written, social-personal, and intercultural). University of Minnesota: Doctoral dissertation.

Winkelman, M. (1994). Cultural shock and adaptation. *Journal of Counseling & Development, 73*(2), 121-126.

Zwingmann, C. A. A. & Gunn, A. D. G. (1983). Uprooting and health: Psychological problems of students from abroad. Geneva: World Health Organization.

APPENDIX

The Experiences and Adjustment Problems of African Questionnaire Form

Directions: Honestly respond to the following questions. Please check or write your Responses.

Part 1 (Background data)

1. Age
____ 18-22 years
____ 23-27 years
____ 28-32 years
____ 33-37 years
____ 38 or more years

2. Gender
____ Male
____ Female

3. Home Country (please write country of citizenship)
   _____

4. What is your classification?
   _____Freshman
   _____sophomore
   _____Junior
   _____Senior
   _____Graduate student

5. What system of education did you go through in your home country?
   _____British system
   _____French system
   _____Spanish system
   _____Other (please specify)_____

6. Did you receive orientation about the American system of education?
   _____Yes
   _____No

7. Did you receive orientation about the American culture (customs, values, And other ways of living)?
   _____Yes
   _____No

8. Where was the orientation received?
   _____Home country
   _____United States
   _____Other (specify)_____

9. How helpful was the orientation?
____Not helpful
____Somewhat helpful
____Helpful
____Very Helpful

10. How do you finance your education while in the United States?
____Delaware State University scholarship or assistantship
____Family and relatives
____U.S. government
____Home government or home institution
____ Other (please specify)

11. How long have you lived in the United States?
____Three months-six months
____Six months-one year
____One year-two years
____Two years-Three years
____Three years-four years
____Four or more years

12. Do you use the DSU counseling services when you experience adjustment problems?
____Never
____Sometimes
____Always

13. How helpful are the counseling services?
____Not helpful
____Somewhat helpful
____Ielpful
____Very Helpful

61

Part 2 (Adjustment problems and the experiences of African students at Delaware State University)

Directions: In the left column of this table is a list of some adjustment problems African students usually face at U.S. colleges. Please check all that apply to you now.

Issues	Not a problem	Somewhat of A problem	Problem	Serious problem
14. Understanding the English language				
15. Familiarity with U. S. customs				
16. Getting acquainted with the U. S. system of education				
17. Getting academic advisement				
18. Understanding Instructors				
19. Experiencing racial and ethnic discrimination				
20. Financing education				

21. Feeling homesick				
22. Feeling lonely				
23. Immigration limitations				
24. Funding healthcare services				
25. Getting used to U.S. foods				
26. Making American friends				
27. Making friends with other international students				

28. How will you rate the services that DSU has in place to help African students adjust? (check one)

____Not adequate

____Somewhat adequate

____Adequate

29. To what extent does your length of stay impact on the level of adjustment problems that you experience? (check one)

____My length of stay has nothing to do with the problems I experience

____My length of stay somewhat has to do with the problems I experience

____My length of stay does have to do with the problems I experience

30. How would you describe your experiences at Delaware State University?
    (check one)

____Not Good

____Somewhat good

____Good

____Very good

____Other (specify)_____